MW01195411

bootstrap

PRODUCT-MARKET FIT
ANALYSIS

BY MATT BROCCHINI

A SECRET WEAPON FOR MARKETERS

bootstrap

Bootstrap Marketing – HQ
1785 San Carlos Ave., Suite 2C   San Carlos, CA 94070

Bootstrap Marketing – SF
135 Main St., Suite 850   San Francisco, CA 94105

+1 (800) 595.4965   (650) 394.4749   info@bootstrap-mktg.com

First Printing, 2015

ISBN-13: 978-1517153625
ISBN-10: 151715362X

Printed in the United States of America

Table of Contents

Product-Market Fit Analysis
Introduction

In 2007, VC Marc Andreessen drew a very simple graphic that changed the way smart start-ups think about their mission. His graphic was a hand-drawn scribble made of two circles and three words: Product – Market – Fit.

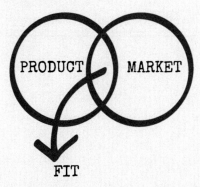

It was in his words: "Only thing that matters for a new start-up".

At Bootstrap Marketing, we agree. Finding product-market fit is what separates successful and struggling start-ups. But how do you find that fit and, in our metric-driven world, how do you measure it?

Using work done by product management experts Chris Sorensen and Matt Brocchini, Bootstrap has developed a quantitative approach that enables companies to assess and improve their product-market fit.

Bootstrap's Product-Market Fit Analysis (PMF Analysis) can be your secret weapon to help get your product and messaging into that product-market fit zone, and keep you there—a step ahead of your competition. We have successfully employed this methodology in our own Customer Discovery and Alignment Workshop and for our clients, and we hope that this guide will help you find similar success.

– Martyn Crew,
Founder & CEO
Bootstrap Marketing

Why You Should Read This Guide

This guide will help you create more effective strategy, positioning, messaging, and content by using the PMF Analysis to clarify the true competitive position and the possible strategic directions of the products you are marketing. Because, after all, marketing is about doing three things:

1) Communicating the competitive advantages of a product

2) Enhancing the competitive advantages of a product

3) Creating new competitive advantages for a product

By uncovering your true competitive advantages, you will be better able to connect the real desires and needs of your target audience with the differentiated advantages of your product, and the better your marketing will perform.

Why Product-Market Fit Analysis?

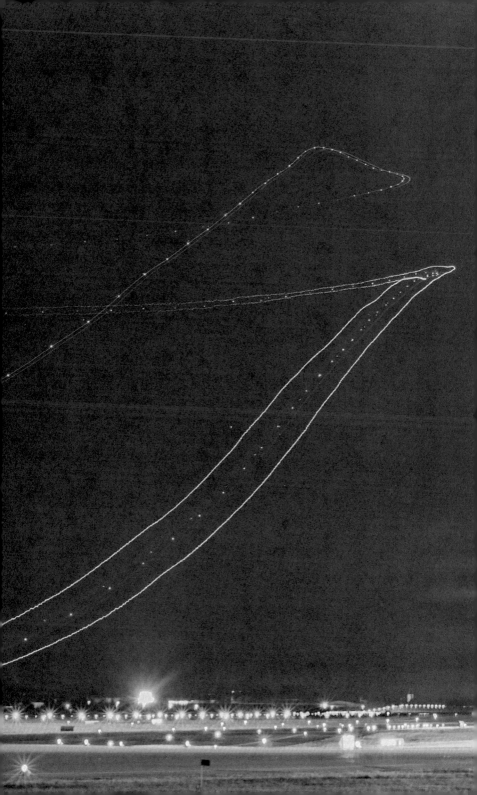

Several years ago after my company was acquired, I joined one of the big Silicon Valley start-up accelerators as an entrepreneur in residence. My job was to listen to start-up pitches, give feedback, and work more intensively with a few clients to help them get from where they were to where they wanted to go.

I loved working with these entrepreneurs. They were smart, engaged, resourceful, and amazingly open-minded people who were just fun to hang out with. But I quickly realized that most of them had a problem: in order to get from where they were to where they wanted to go, they needed to know two things:

1) Where they were, and

2) Where they wanted to go

Sounds simple, right? But it's not simple. A start-up's job is to create a new product that a lot of people will buy. Start-ups operate in a complex environment—different market segments have different needs, existing products are evolving rapidly, and other start-ups are chasing the same opportunities. It is a high-stakes game, and every player is working with partial information. It is complex enough that members of the same team frequently have very different assumptions and beliefs about those two basic questions.

So I asked myself, "How can I help these teams develop a solid, shared concept of their core value proposition?"

Luckily for me, I didn't have to come up with the answer on my own. My fellow entrepreneur in residence, Chris Sorensen, was struggling

with the same issue, and he realized that the solution had to be based on a clear-eyed assessment of product-market fit. I asked Chris, "What kills most start-ups?" He replied, "Running out of money before achieving product-market fit."

So together we got to work on a process to help our start-ups develop a clear, shared, actionable vision of where they are and where they need to go to succeed.

We wanted something that would include these elements:

1) Who is my product for?

2) What's most important to those people?

3) What are their alternatives to buying my product?

4) How does my product stack up against the alternatives?

5) What could happen to erode my competitive advantage?
   What do I need to watch out for?

6) What can I do to increase my competitive advantage?
   What should my strategy be?

Over the course of a few months, we refined this into the strategic framework that we call Quantitative Product-Market Fit. We designed it to mentor start-ups in the art of profitable innovation. It worked, and we continue to use it today to help both start-ups and enterprise product teams optimize their product strategies.

Product-Market Fit: A Magnetic Force

Remember when Cinderella slid her foot into the glass slipper? She found that the dimensions of her foot and the dimensions of the shoe were a perfect match.

Product-market fit is the level of match between what customers want and what a product provides. It is a magnetic force that attracts and binds customers to products. The better the fit, the higher the market share, the more loyal customers tend to be, and the more difficult it is for a competitor to lure customers away.

- High fit means low customer acquisition cost, high loyalty, and high lifetime customer value.
- Low fit means high customer churn, high customer acquisition costs, and low loyalty.

It really is like a magnet: in one polarity it attracts customers, and in the other it repels them.

Marc Andreessen put it very well:

"You can always feel product/market fit when it's happening. The customers are buying the product just as fast as you can make it—or usage is growing just as fast as you can add more servers.

Money from customers is piling up in your company checking account. You're hiring sales and customer support staff as fast as you can. Reporters are calling because they've heard about your hot new thing and they want to talk to you about it."

– Marc Andreessen

However, recognizing it when you have it is one thing; achieving it is another. And it's not just about having the right product. It's also about marketing it to the right people in the right way.

That's why marketers can use the Quantitative Product-Market Fit framework as a secret weapon. It can help you find the market segments where your product has the greatest advantage, and it can help you determine what messages are most likely to drive sales in those segments.

The following will describe how to quantify product-market fit by looking at the Customer Value Model (what customers want) and Product Performance (what the product provides). The precision of the fit between the two is the Quantitative Product-Market Fit.

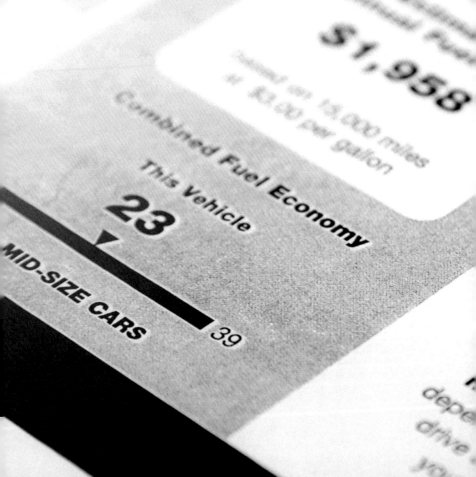

What Your Customers Care About

Economy Estimates

HIGHWAY MPG

30

Expected range
for most drivers
24 to **36** MPG

Your actual
will var

The Customer Value Model describes what customers care about when they are considering buying a product. The things they care about are labeled as Value Dimensions. For example, if the product category is automobiles, the Value Dimensions might include:

- Price
- Performance
- Prestige
- Capacity
- Fuel Economy
- Comfort

The second component of the Customer Value Model is the relative importance of these Value Dimensions, known as the "weight" of each dimension. The weight of each Value Dimension indicates how big a role it plays in purchase behavior by customers in that segment. This can be depicted graphically:

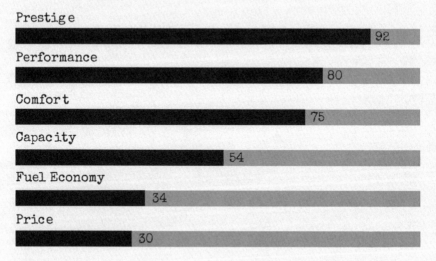

Prestige
92

Performance
80

Comfort
75

Capacity
54

Fuel Economy
34

Price
30

At a glance, you can tell that this Value Model is for a luxury car customer segment, as Prestige and Performance are the Value Dimensions with the highest weight, whereas Fuel Economy and Price don't matter much to customers in this segment.

Delivering On Your Customers' Needs

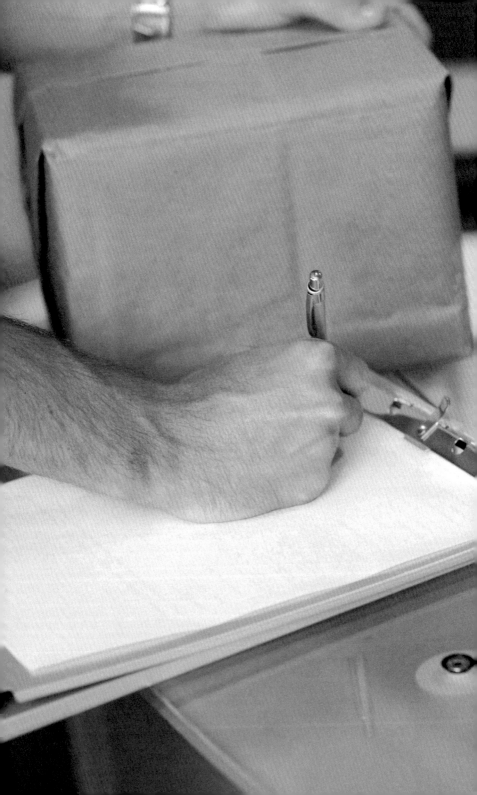

Product Performance is a measure of how well specific products deliver on the Value Dimensions in the Customer Value Model. This can be depicted graphically in the same way:

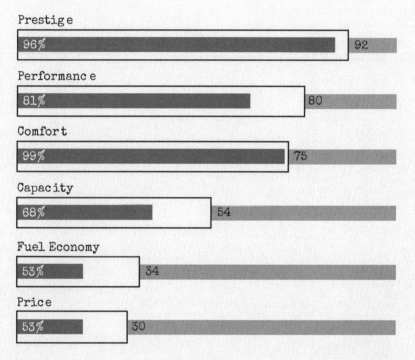

The orange bars represent how well a particular product performs in each Value Dimension. Overall, this product looks pretty good. In the Comfort Dimension, the fit is almost perfect. It also does well in the primary Value Dimensions of *Prestige* and *Performance*. Its *Capacity*, *Fuel Economy*, and *Price* are not great, but those are less important for this segment.

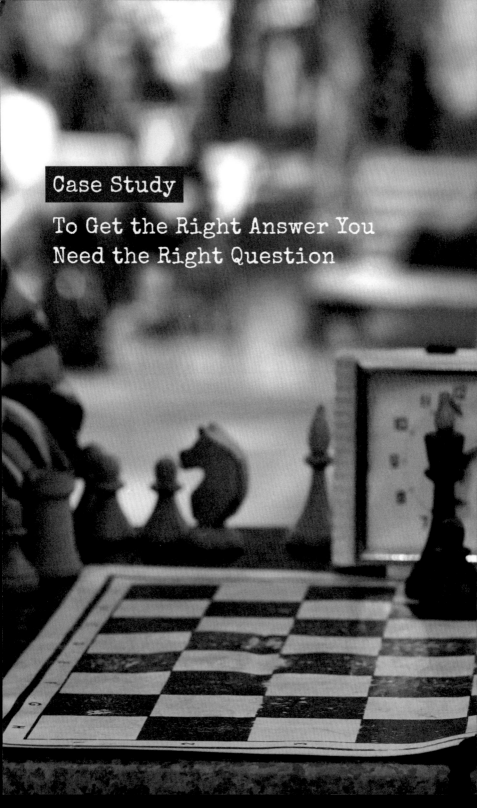

Case Study

To Get the Right Answer You
Need the Right Question

Case Study

One of the most valuable aspects of the PMF Analysis is that it quickly reveals your assumptions about what's important to your customers, how well your product or service delivers on those customer needs and desires, and how you stack up against the competition. And with the assumptions out in the open, you can take action. A prime example of this can be seen in Bootstrap Marketing's implementation of the PMF Analysis.

In early 2015 the Bootstrap team went through a PMF Analysis to uncover assumptions about their own product-market fit. They wanted to explore a particular type of Bootstrap customer: technology start-ups that are moving into their growth stage and need to execute a launch that will quickly build awareness and revenue. These tend to be companies that have established a strong need for their product with a small number of customers, but are still relatively unknown to the majority of their target customers.

Bootstrap has an excellent track record helping start-ups like this develop launch strategies that deliver results. But what they wanted to better understand was what these start-ups look for in a marketing partner.

In an accelerated two-hour session, we went through the analysis and defined the key Value Dimensions for the segment, selected a set of competitors to evaluate, and scored everything. Because the PMF Analysis process forced the Bootstrap team to quantitatively rank every Value Dimension in terms of how important it is to their customers and how well they and their competitors perform, it immediately revealed interesting results.

First, the process revealed that Bootstrap's two primary competitors are virtually identical in terms of how they appear to customers.

Second, it revealed that when start-ups are about to launch and are looking for a partner to help them do it, there are two main qualities they look for:

> **Strategy** – Given the complexity of the communication challenges that disruptive start-ups face, they need an experienced team that understands how to focus marketing energy on the right audience and craft a positioning and messaging strategy that will inspire customers to take action.

> **Marketing execution** – Start-ups need a partner that can deliver high-quality marketing content and programs quickly and efficiently.

The team agreed that strategy and execution were the two most important Value Dimensions; however, the PMF Analysis uncovered a question the Bootstrap team could not answer with confidence: "What do our customers value more? Our strategic capability or our marketing execution skills?"

So they did what smart marketers do—they asked the customer. A survey went out, and the results came in: the clear message that customers deeply value is Bootstraps ability to help start-ups with BOTH developing an effective strategy AND skillfully executing marketing programs.

With this knowledge of what their customers value, Bootstrap has dramatically improved communications with their audience.

The PMF Analysis led them to the right question; the question led them to the right answer.

Case Study

Beauty Is in the Eye of the Beholder

Case Study

Beauty, they say, is in the eye of the beholder. Do you know what your customers see when they look at your product? And do you know how the view varies from customer to customer?

A client of ours asked us to help with the positioning, messaging, and launch of a new product. Their customers are in the oil and gas industry: the drillers who get the goods out of the ground and into the pipelines that move it across the continent, the processors who turn it into the fuels, and the utility companies that deliver it to our homes to light our stoves and heat our houses. Their product is a disruptive cloud-based entrant into a market populated with old-school solutions that are slow to deploy and expensive to maintain. So they felt they knew what the positioning should be: "Tired of your old creaky solution? Save time and money with _____."

Positioning is a high-stakes game. It is the foundation of your marketing messaging. Get it right and it drives the performance of your website, direct campaigns, social presence, and sales activities. Get it wrong and you run the risk of being ignored—or worse.

So to double-check our client's assumption regarding their positioning, we took the team through a two-day Quantitative Product-Market Fit process. On day one we laid out the key Value Dimensions for each of their customer segments. These turned out to be Compliance, Reliability, Speed of Deployment, Configurability, Total Cost of Ownership, Ease of Use, and a few others. Then we gave each of these an "importance" score, for each market segment. By the end of the day we had a detailed Customer Value Model for each of their seven most important customer segments. Armed with this quantitative view of what matters to their customers, we could move onto the next step.

On day two we scored our client's product and eight of the most important competitors. These included both other products and alternatives such as homegrown solutions. Working together, we scored our client's product and each competitive solution for all customer segments.

The results? Some important insights that led us to re-think the positioning and messaging strategy for their product launch.

The most important overall theme to emerge was that their customers are operating in an industry that is in the midst of rapid change. Everything from new drilling technologies to regulatory changes to unpredictable weather is shaking things up. For these companies, opportunities appear quickly and must be acted on right away; and the same goes for problems. This means our client's primary advantage is not cost savings or faster deployment. Both are important, but adaptability and configurability are even more important to their customers. This insight eventually led us to positioning based on these advantages, and messaging built around a simple statement: "Change Happens. Be Ready with _____."

We also found that there are important groupings of market segments, in terms of which of our client's advantages are most important. For example, our client's advantages are very similar for both Utilities and Pipelines segments: Configurability, Reliability, and Support. Similar overall messaging will resonate for customers in both of these segments.

In contrast, the Customer Value Models and their advantages are quite different for the Gathering and Plant Processing segments. The messaging that works for Utilities is not going to work for Plant Processing.

Knowing this, we were able to avoid two mistakes: first, using generic messaging with customers who are not likely to respond to it, and second, wasting time and money on differentiated messaging for segments that don't need it. If you know what your various customer segments care about, you can group them and make the most of your investment in content and creative.

Before committing to product positioning and building your marketing messaging around it, it pays to take a look at your product through your customer's eyes.

Case Study

The Shoe Doesn't Fit? Maybe You
Need a Different Foot

Case Study

If your product does not have the degree of product-market fit that it needs to be truly successful, most of the time the solution is to improve the product—but not always. Sometimes, what you need are different customers. Here's an example from my own experience.

In 2005, I became the EVP of Technology & Operations at Nimblefish, a San Francisco start-up and a pioneer in cross-channel marketing automation. Our product let marketers build amazing omni-channel campaigns utilizing email, personalized websites, and digitally printed direct mail, all with content specifically targeted to the individual customer. You might remember the buzz-phrase "1:1 marketing" which was circulating at that time—that's what we were really good at; big campaigns with lots of online and offline components and millions of variations in messaging.

The product generated outstanding results for customers. For example, in a big product launch for Apple, we helped them generate 11 times greater response and conversion than their typical direct marketing campaign. Our campaigns did cost more to run, about two to three times as much as a typical direct campaign, but the ROI was huge. Invest 3x more, get back 11x more? I'll take it!

But, there was a catch. These campaigns also required a lot more work from the marketers. In order to generate highly targeted messaging we needed detailed information about the desires and pain points of a dozen or more market micro-segments, and we needed Apple's marketing team to provide it for us. This was more work than they were used to doing for a campaign. So even though the campaign produced huge ROI, the team was exhausted. The general reaction was, "That was fantastic! But let's not do it again—at least not now. We need a break!"

So, what could we do? Since the power of the campaigns were largely due to the precision targeting of the messaging, we really did need the marketers to provide detailed information about their customer segments. We could make product changes that would reduce the workload a little, but the problem was not going away. So we asked ourselves, "What if we could find a customer who was more willing to put in the work, maybe because the payoff was bigger?" And "Could we find a new set of customers where our current product, with no changes, had a higher quantitative product-market fit?"

The answer was yes, and we found them. The first of these new customers was Lowe's, the giant home improvement retailer, who used our product to target people who were remodeling their kitchens. The products and messaging for kitchen remodels don't change much from year to year, and people don't remodel their kitchens very often. That meant that the messaging for the campaign could be used year-over-year with minimal updates. So the return on the work they did setting up the messaging was much higher.

Lowes was followed by many other companies as diverse as Invisalign and Marriott Vacation Club. But what they all had in common was that they were selling a considered purchase product, the product didn't change very often, and customers didn't buy frequently—you don't remodel your kitchen, get cosmetic braces, or buy a timeshare vacation home very often. So it was fine for the company to use essentially the same messaging for years, especially if it is precisely targeted to each customer.

This change had a massive impact for Nimblefish. We went from an average deal size of about $75,000 to over $1,000,000, and each deal produced recurring revenue for years. Our company grew by 10x and we were acquired a few years later.

Putting it into Practice

Now that you're familiar with the PMF Analysis framework and how it has made an impact at other companies, it's time for you to try doing this for your product. The following three-step process will help you learn a lot about your product and your own assumptions.

Step 1: Define the most important market segment—what group of customers is the most valuable to you?

Step 2: List the top 5 Value Dimensions for that segment—what is most important to those customers when they are considering a product like yours? Then give each dimension a value between 0 and 100 based on the level of importance. Force yourself to score it.

Step 3: Estimate your product's performance in each dimension—how well does your product meet your customers' needs and desires? Score your product on a scale of 0-100 in each dimension. Again, force yourself to give each dimension a number.

PMF Analysis: _____
(Product Name)

SEGMENT:				

TOP 5 VALUE DIMENSIONS				

VALUE DIMENSION WEIGHT				

PERFORMANCE				

Use the following chart to define the weight of a Value Dimension and its impact on purchase behavior.

Value Dimension Weight	Impact on Purchase Behavior
0	**Irrelevant.** This dimension has no value to customers.
1-30	**Not very important.** Has a small impact on buying decisions. Performance in this dimension is unlikely to drive purchase behavior unless two products are in very close neck-and-neck competition.
30-60	**Moderately Important.**
70-100	**Highly important.** These are the value dimensions that will have the greatest impact on purchase behavior.

If this is hard to do, it shows that you're not as clear as you need to be about what your customers care about and why they would choose your product. If it's easy, it will lay your assumptions on the table for further examination and testing.

If you have great product-market fit, it will show you how to tune your messaging to have the highest impact. If the fit is not that great, it will show you where you need to improve (or it might mean that you should target a different customer segment where the fit is better).

Either way, you're a step ahead of most marketers. You've taken the first steps toward having an analytical picture of your product's true advantages and weaknesses. With this strategic foundation, you'll create marketing messaging that works.

Closing Remarks

A beautiful website and brilliant social marketing campaigns are not going to deliver if they don't reach the right people or carry the right message. Furthermore, in order to stand out in an increasingly crowded marketplace, it's never been more critical that you identify, leverage, and effectively communicate your true differentiated advantages.

Bootstrap's Product-Market Fit Analysis provides an innovative, effective and quick way to help you reveal valuable insight into your customers' needs and how your product stacks up against those needs. Having this knowledge will lead to better business results by developing messaging around what your customers care about, not what looks cool or sounds clever.

Now, let's find the foot that's a perfect match for your "glass slipper."

About the Author

Matt Brocchini is a technology & education entrepreneur and executive. He was a founder or early exec in 6 tech start-ups, with one IPO and one acquisition. After his early days as Director of Product Management at Oracle he founded Helium.com, an innovation consulting firm that designed and built ground-breaking products for clients ranging from Adobe to the San Francisco 49ers to AXA Investment Management. Helium later merged with Nimblefish Technologies, which was sold to RR Donnelley in 2010. Matt is a founding board member and current Board Chair of the Institute for Applied Tinkering, a non-profit that operates Brightworks and Tinkering School and whose mission is fostering innovation in children.

About Bootstrap

Bootstrap Marketing is a full-service, digital marketing agency with deep expertise in start-up and high-growth marketing.

Our team is made up of experienced software marketing professionals with deep backgrounds in marketing, business development, research, and graphic and website design.

Based in San Carlos, CA, we serve companies in Silicon Valley, the San Francisco Bay Area and beyond, including European, Asian and Pacific Rim companies taking their first steps into the U.S. market.

We believe that in today's mobile and web-based 24x7 marketing world, ideas and campaigns must be brought to market quickly, and must be agile and adaptable to meet the needs and expectations of today's business consumer. And to do that, we believe you need a smart, fast, responsive, and scalable marketing partner—Bootstrap Marketing.

Stay Connected

Visit bootstrap-mktg.com
Follow @bootstrapmktg
Join the Conversation #ASKBOOTSTRAP

Bootstrap Marketing – HQ

1785 San Carlos Ave., Suite 2C
San Carlos, CA 94070

Bootstrap Marketing – SF

135 Main St., Suite 850
San Francisco, CA 94105

+1 (650) 394-4749

info@bootstrap-mktg.com